I0485592

Mystical

Mandala Coloring book

By

S.B. Nozaz

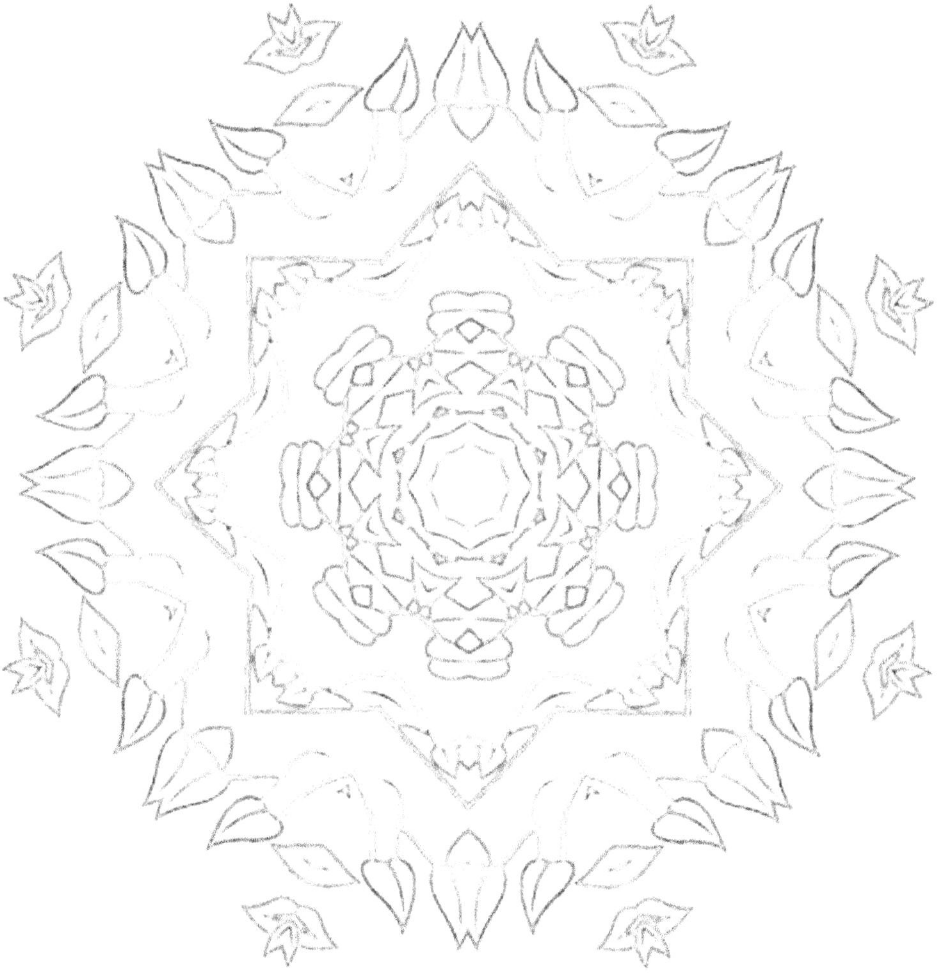

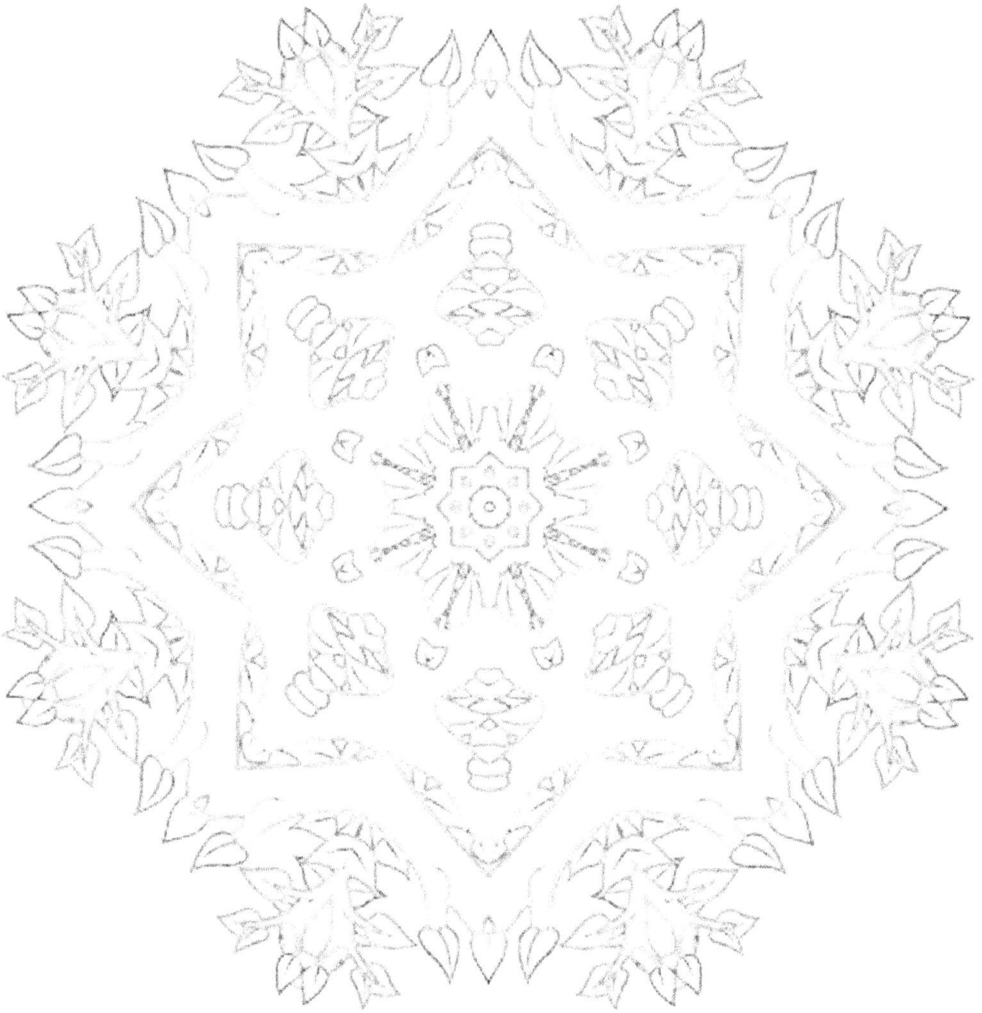

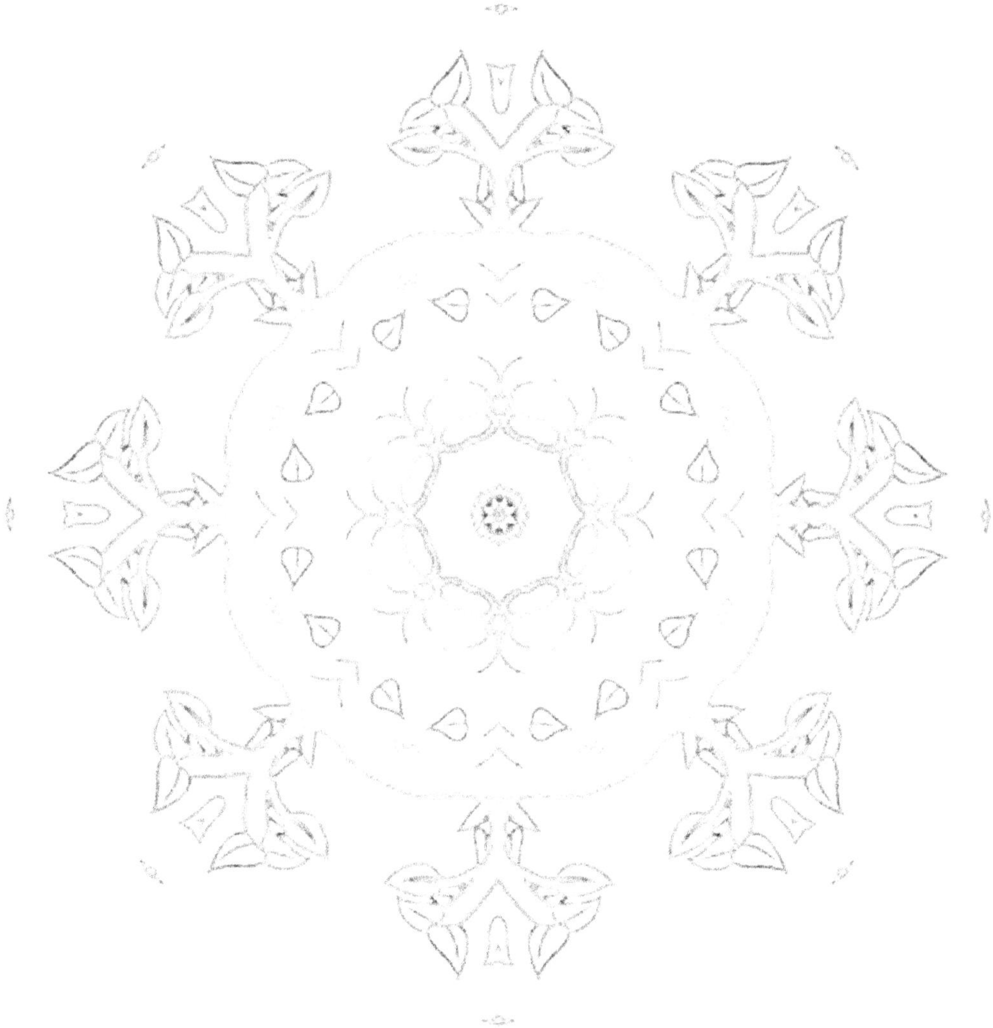

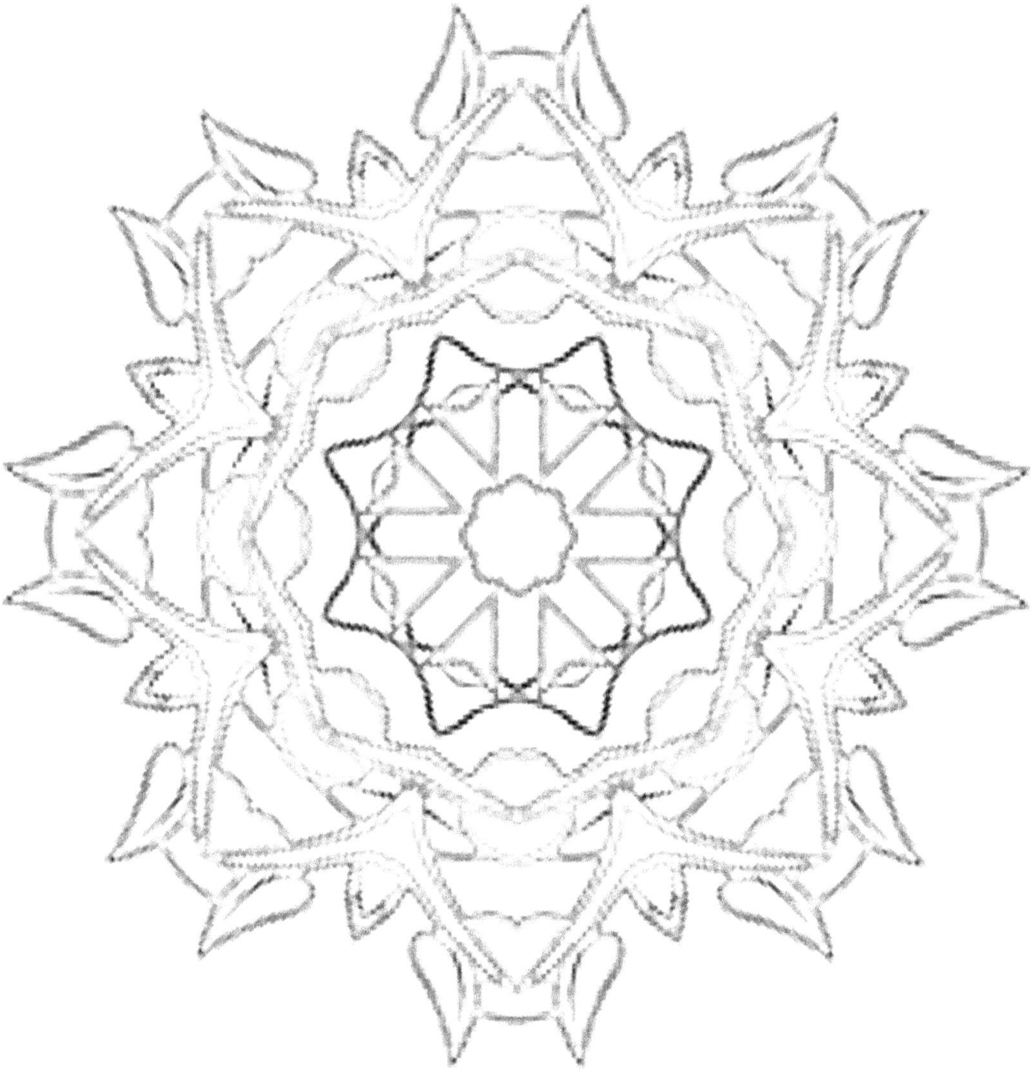

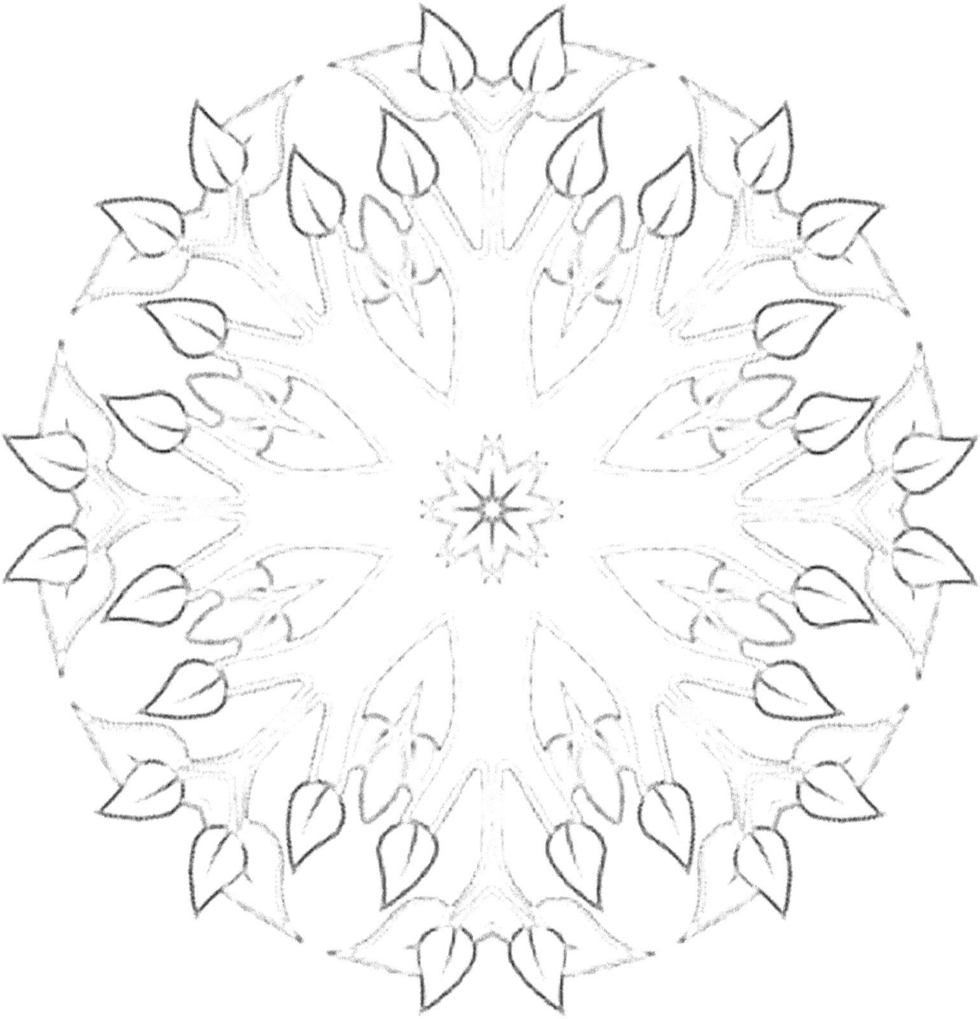

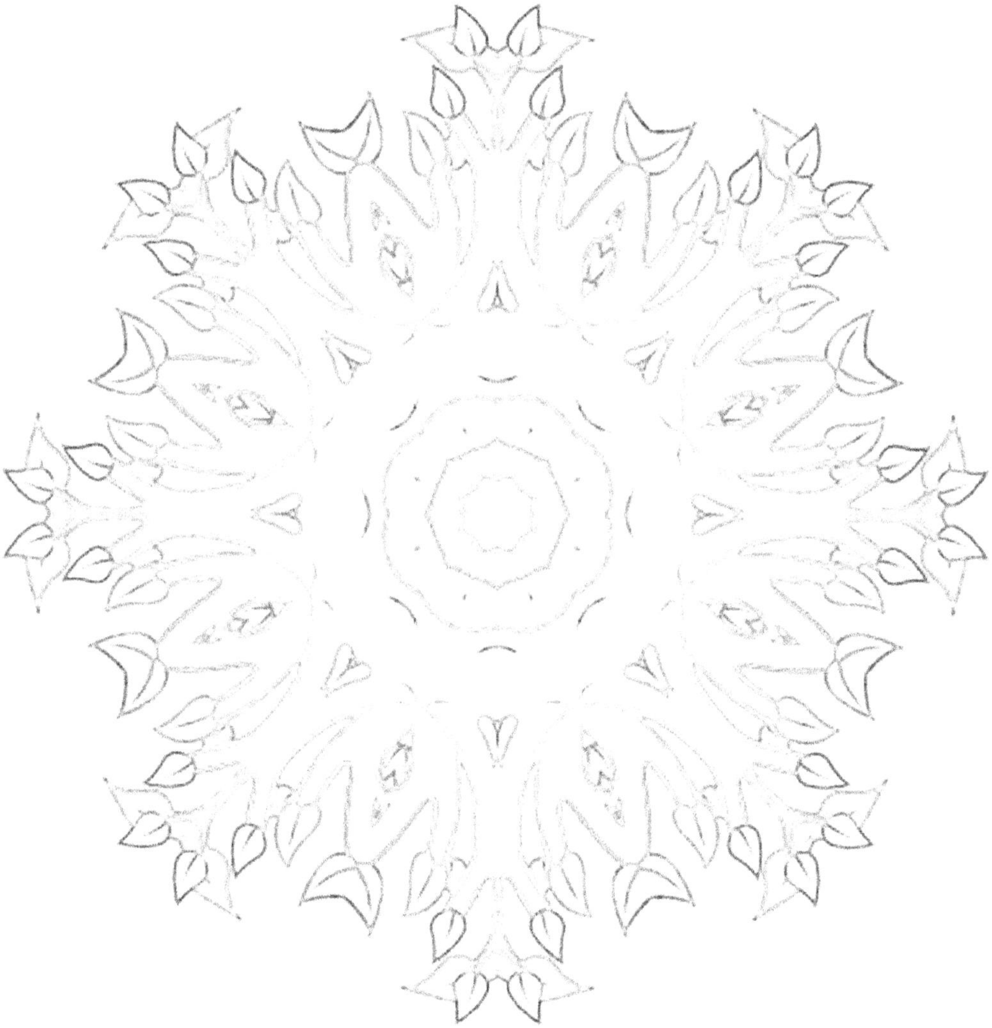

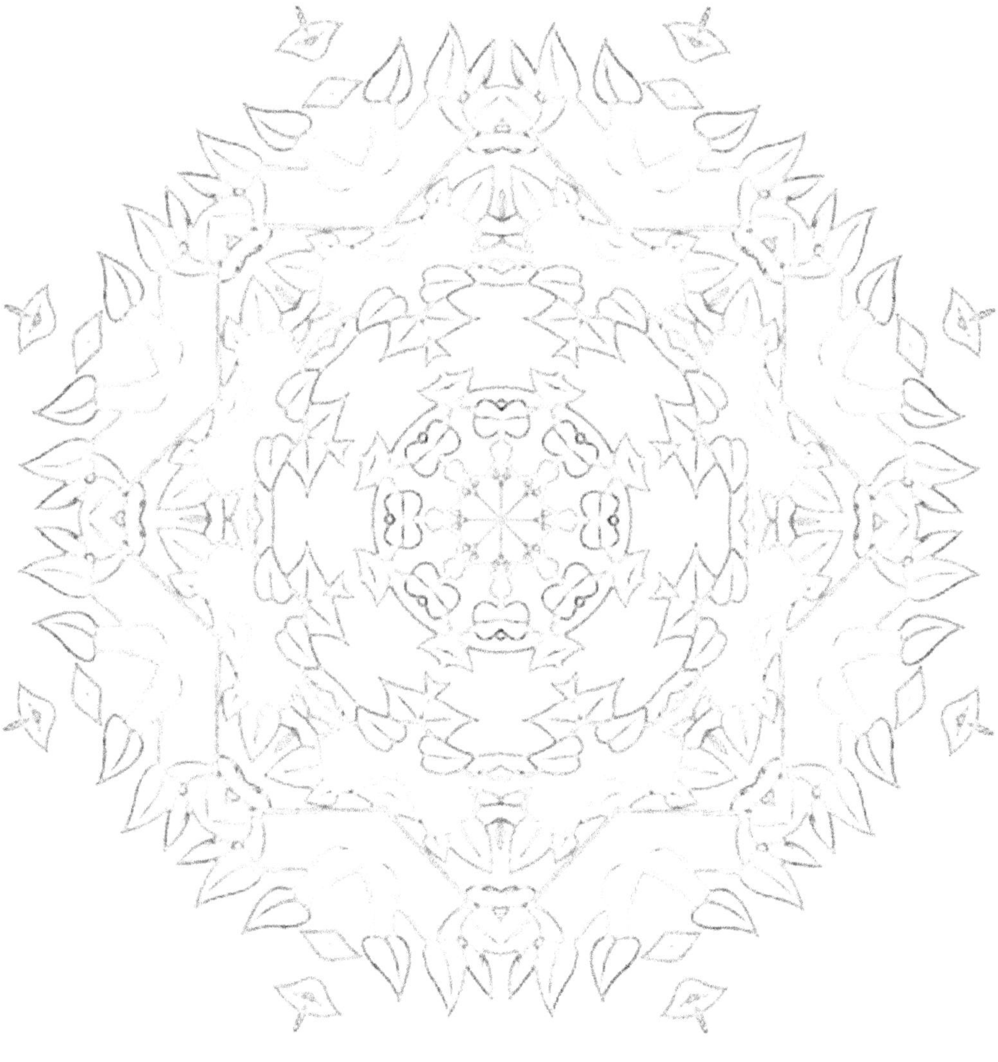

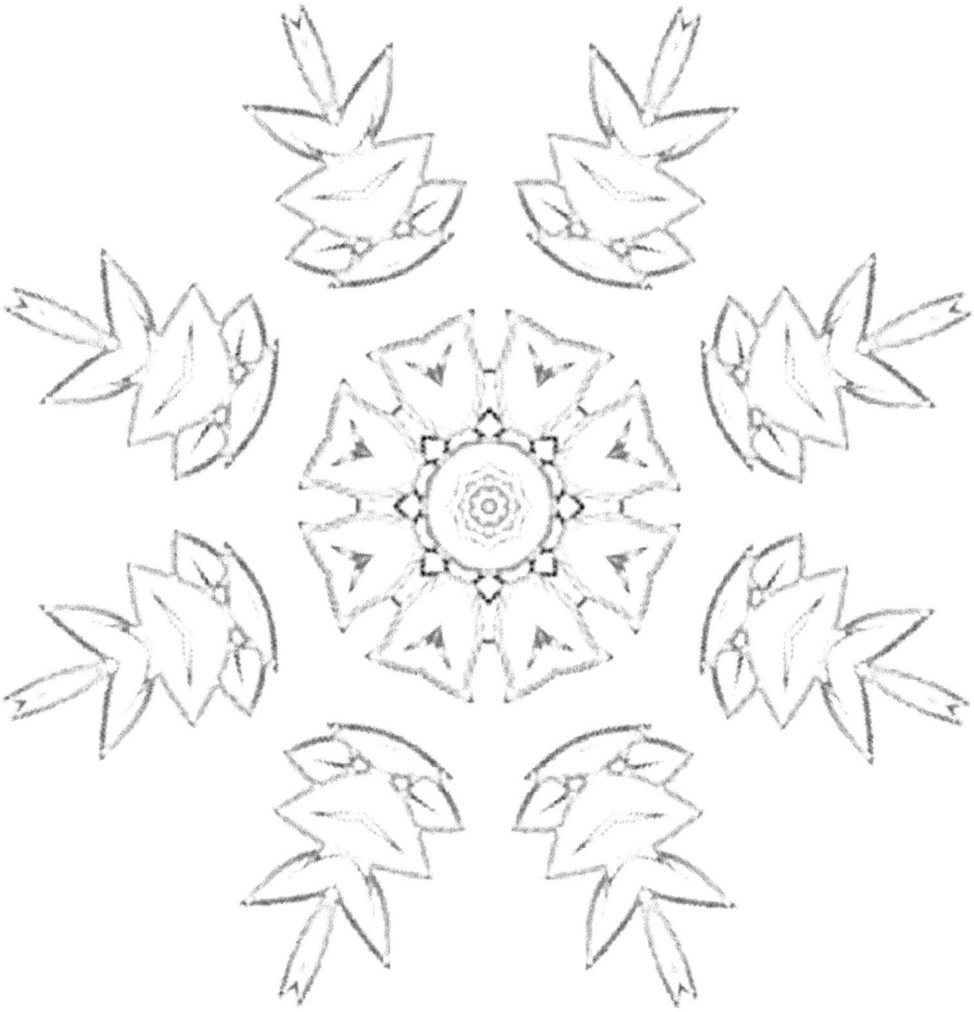

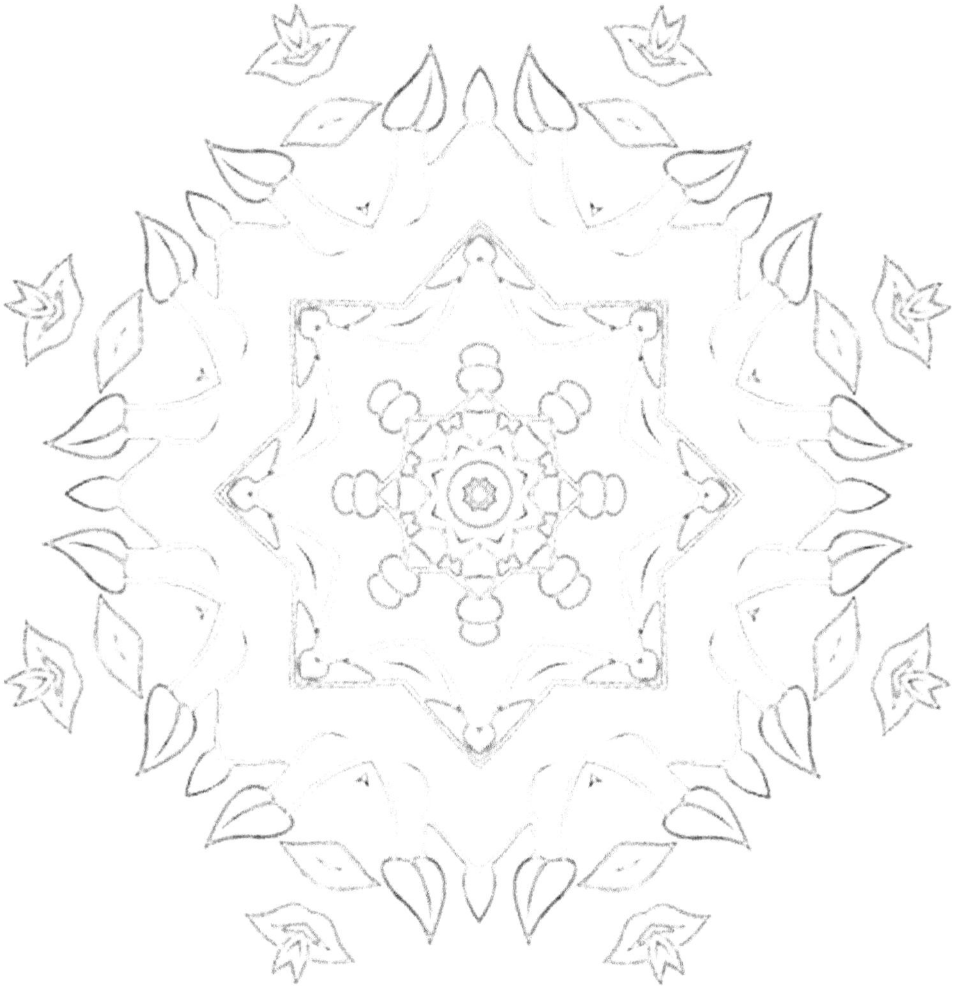

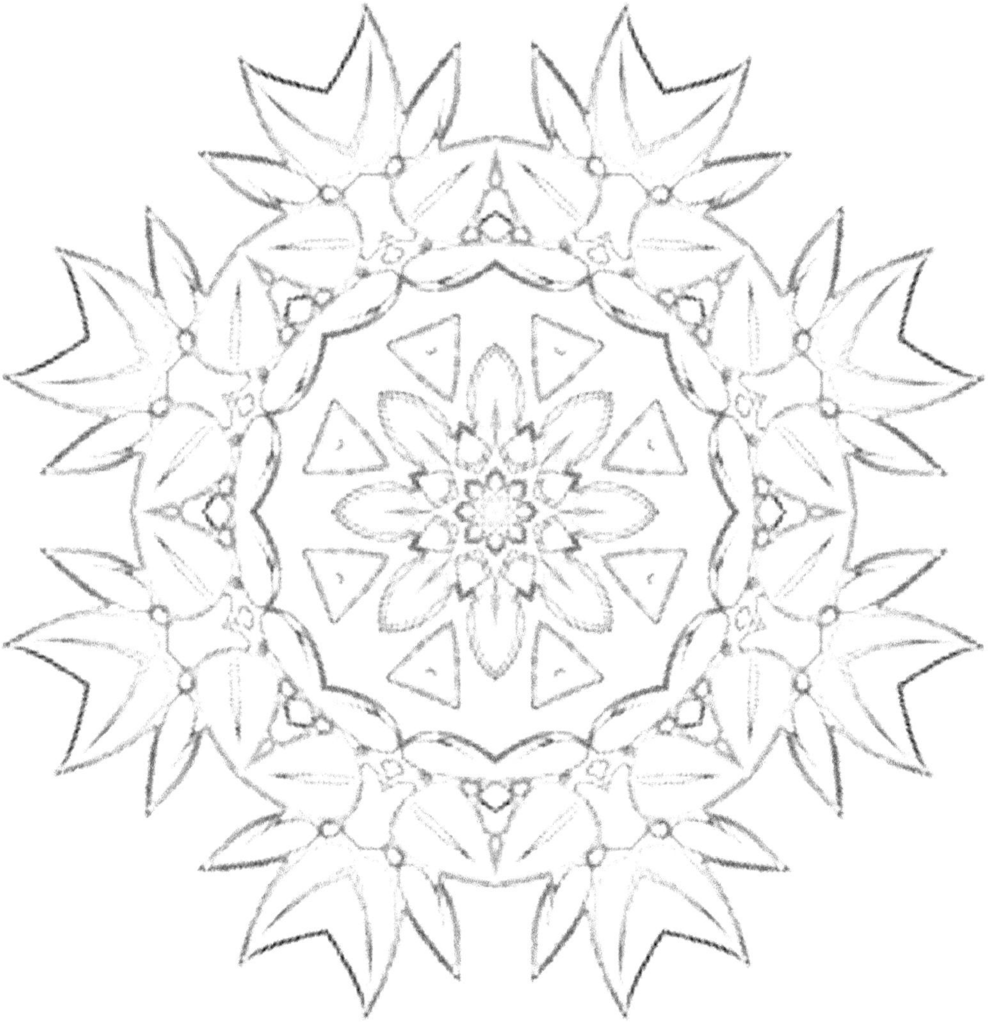

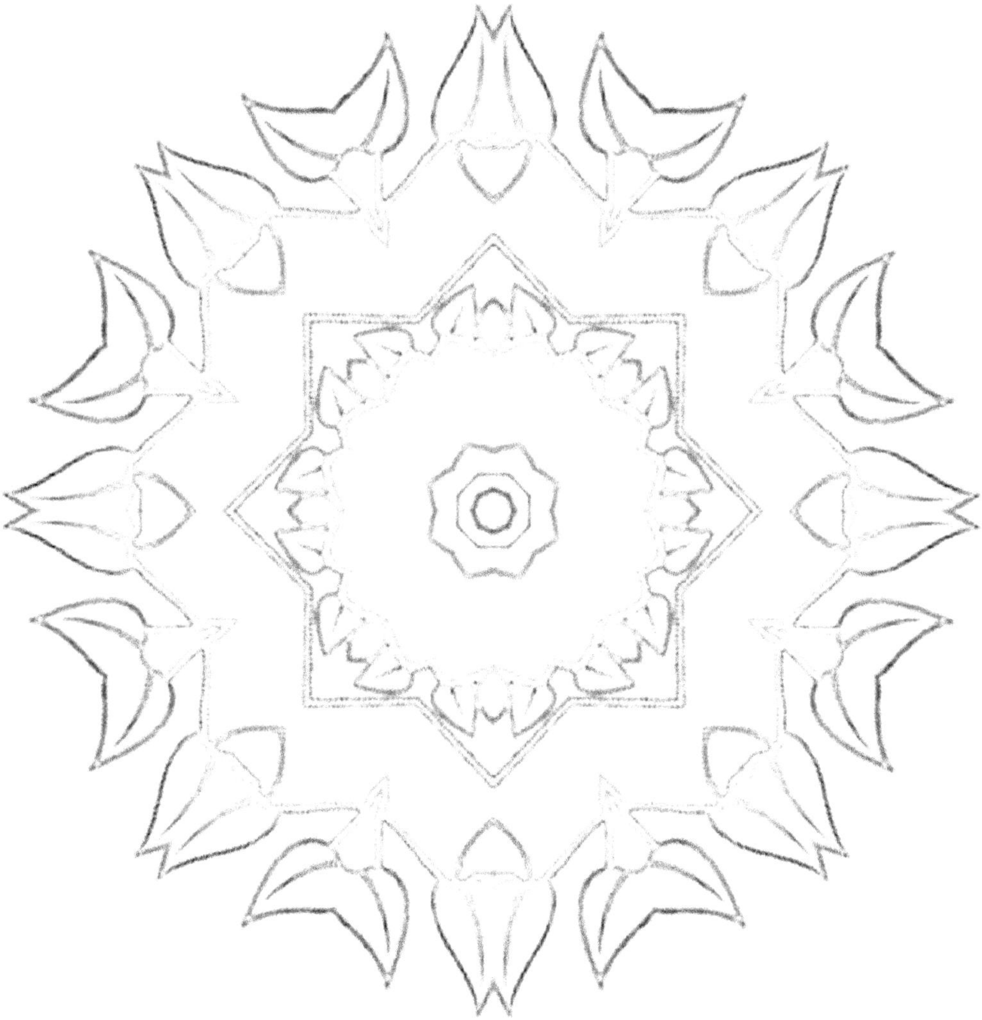

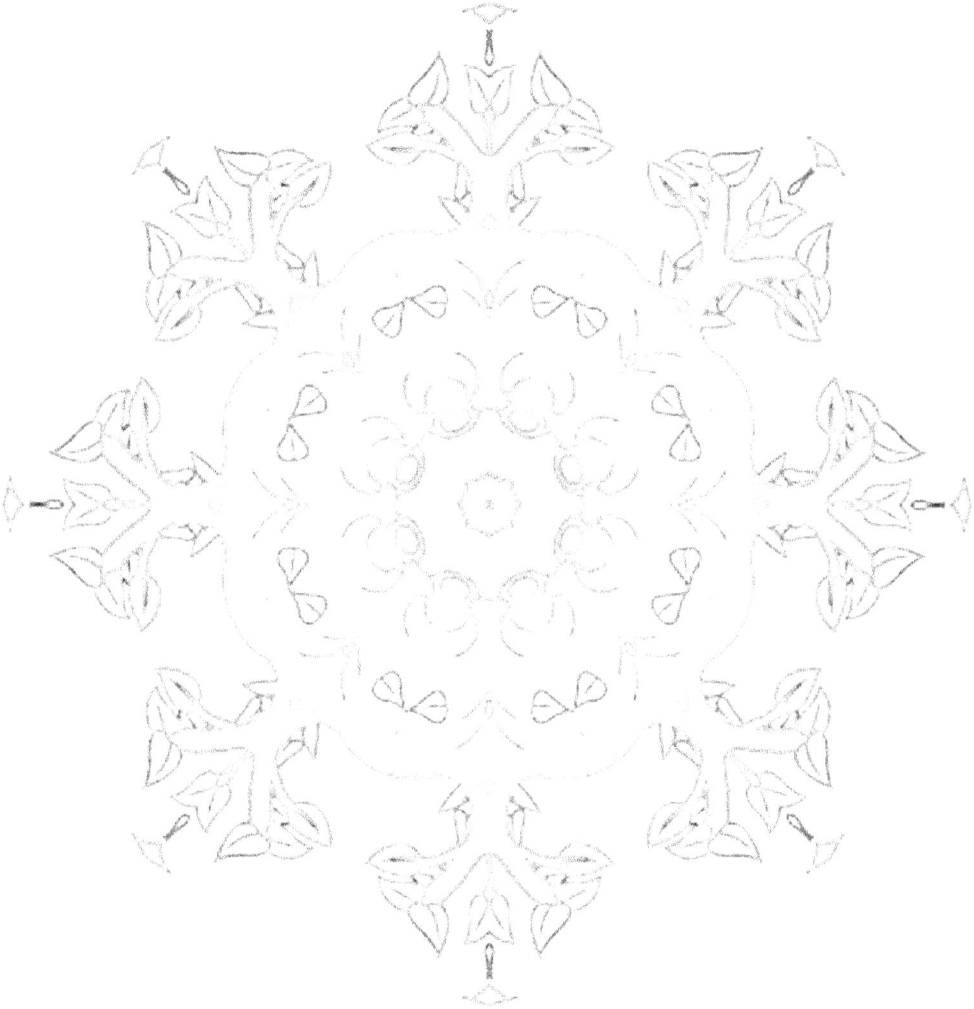

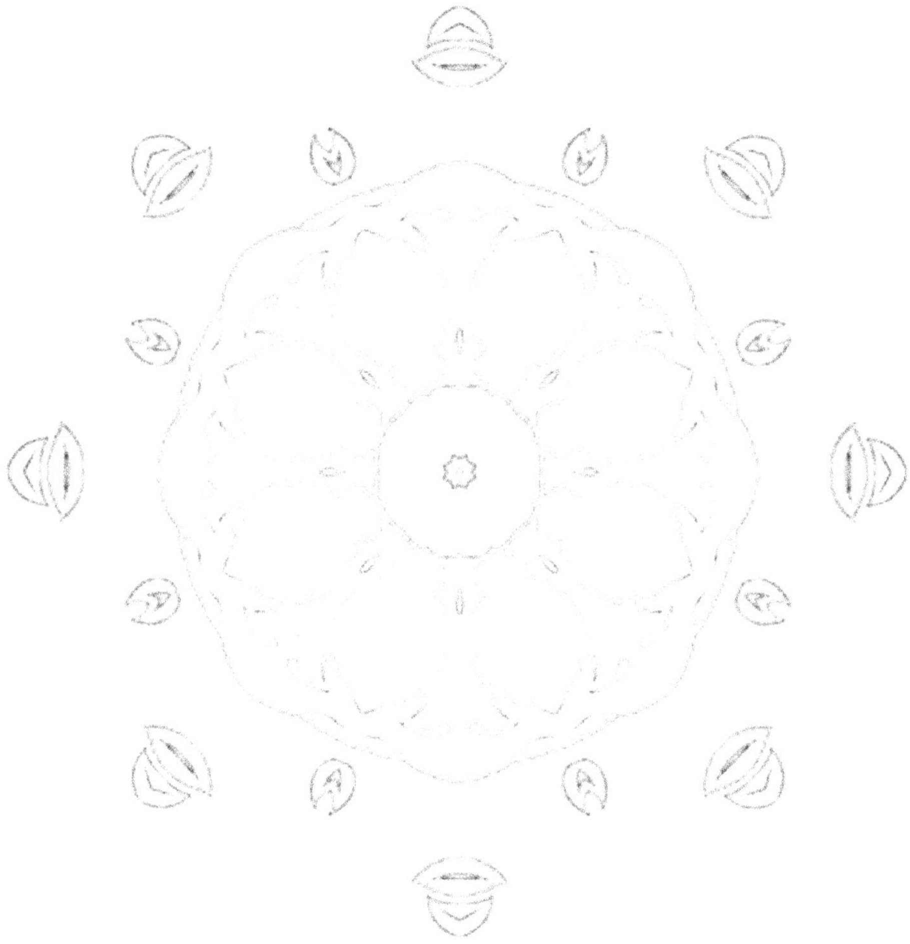

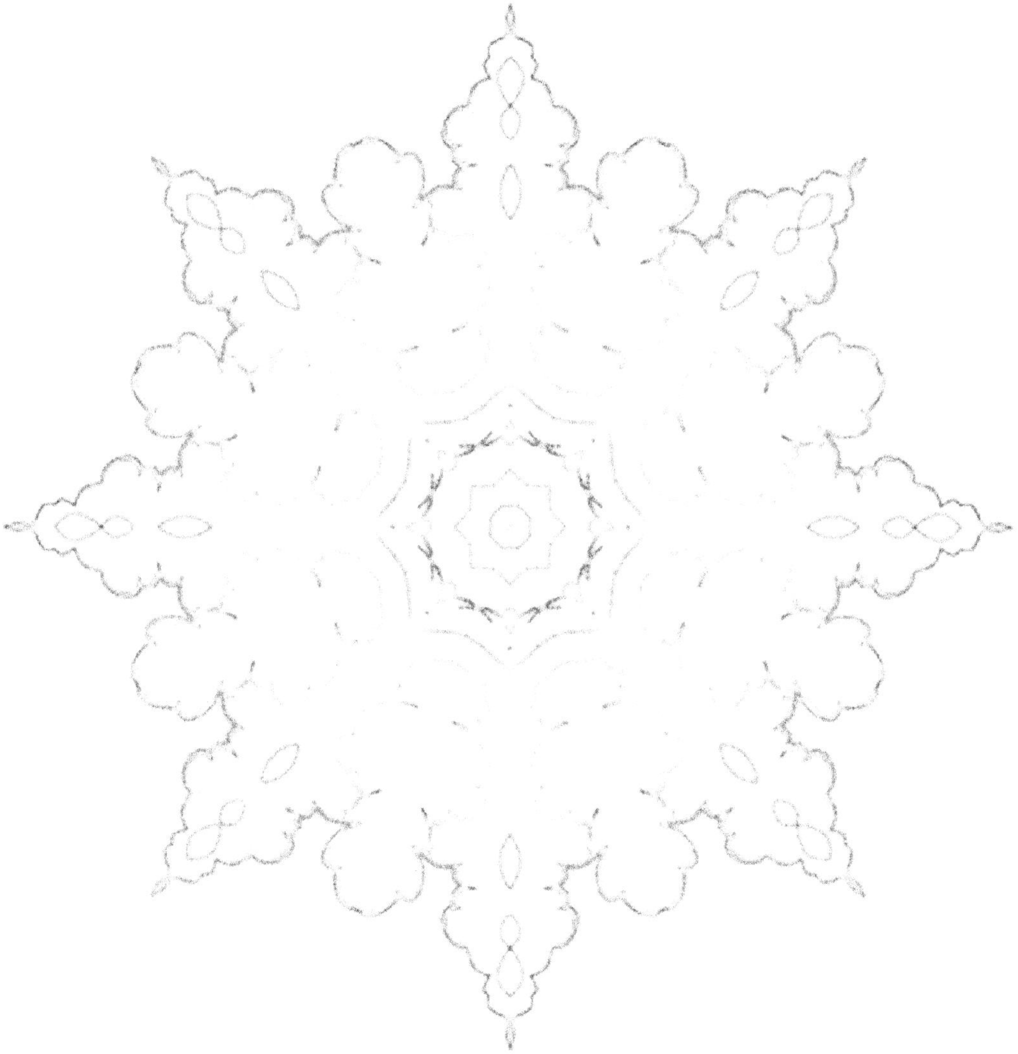

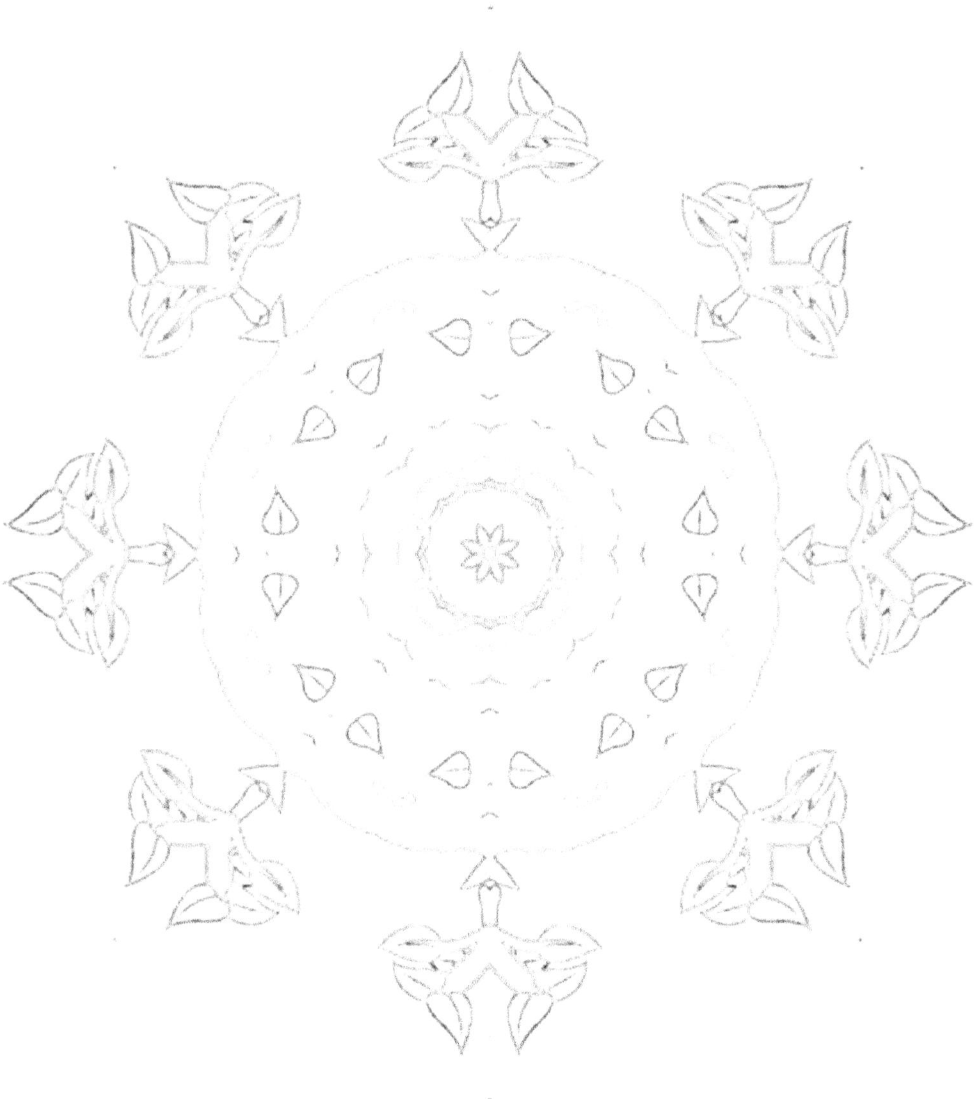

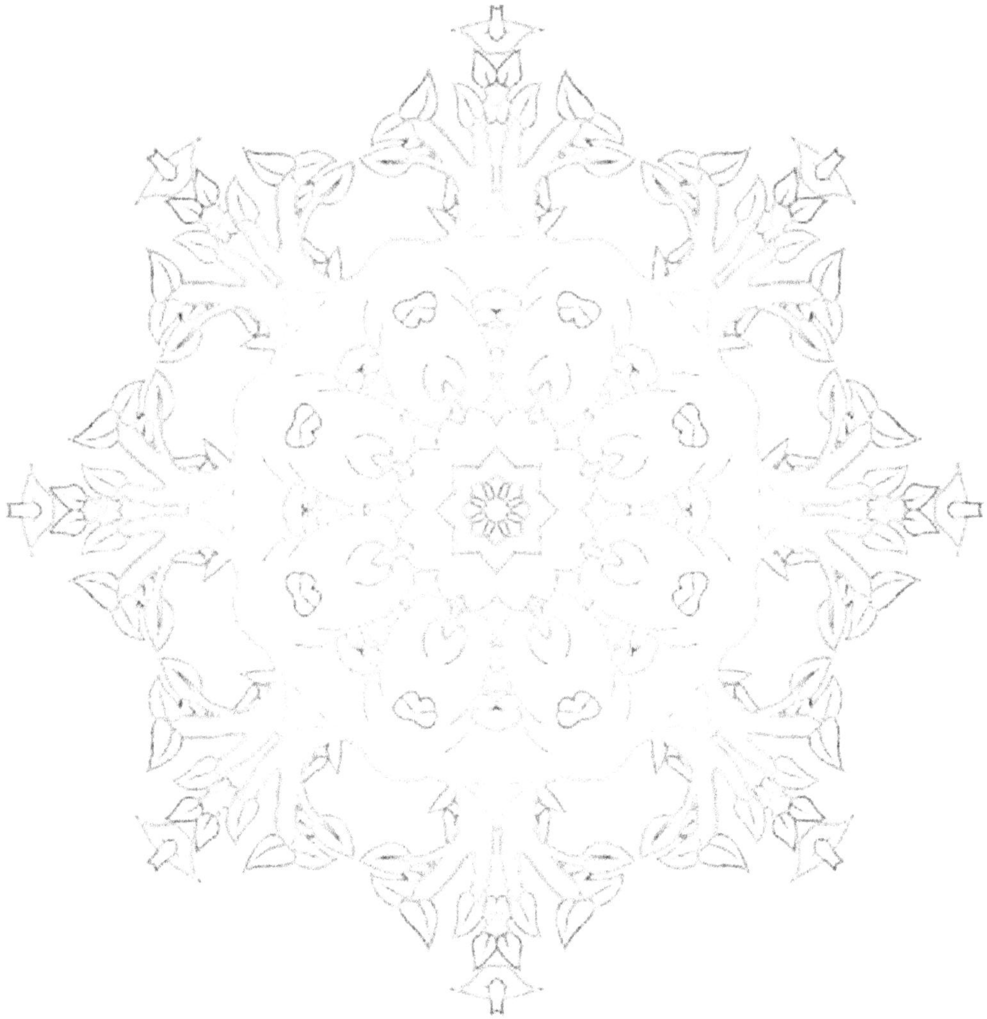

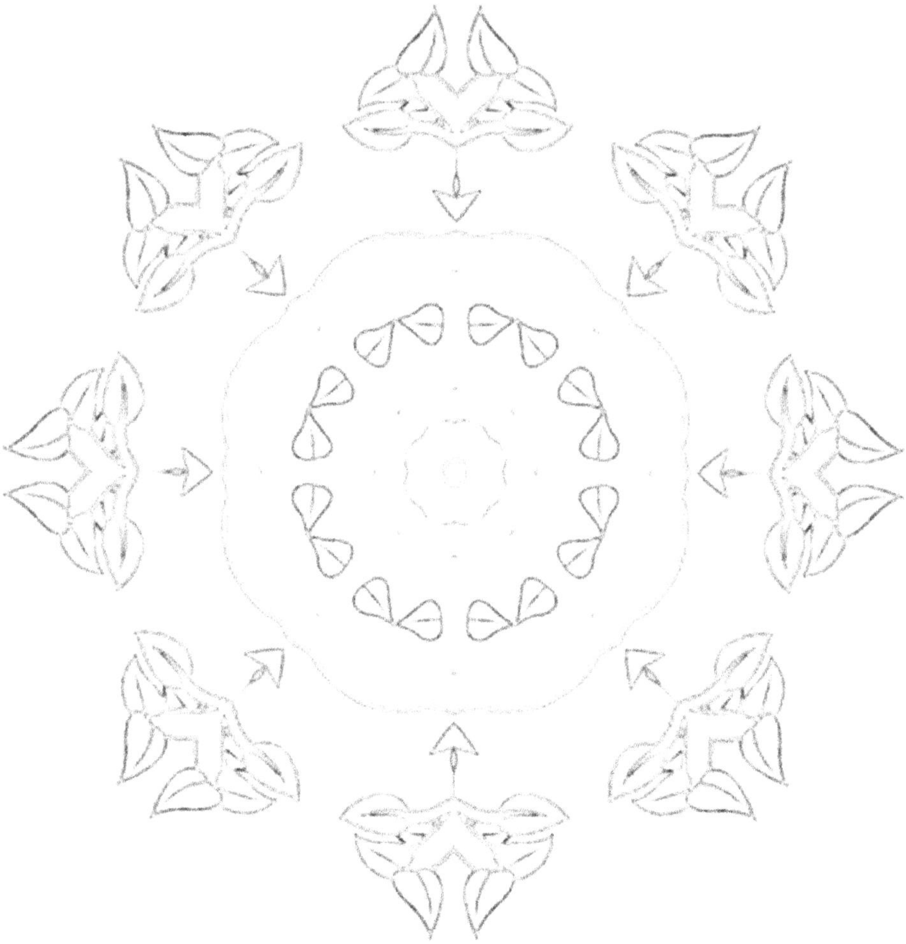

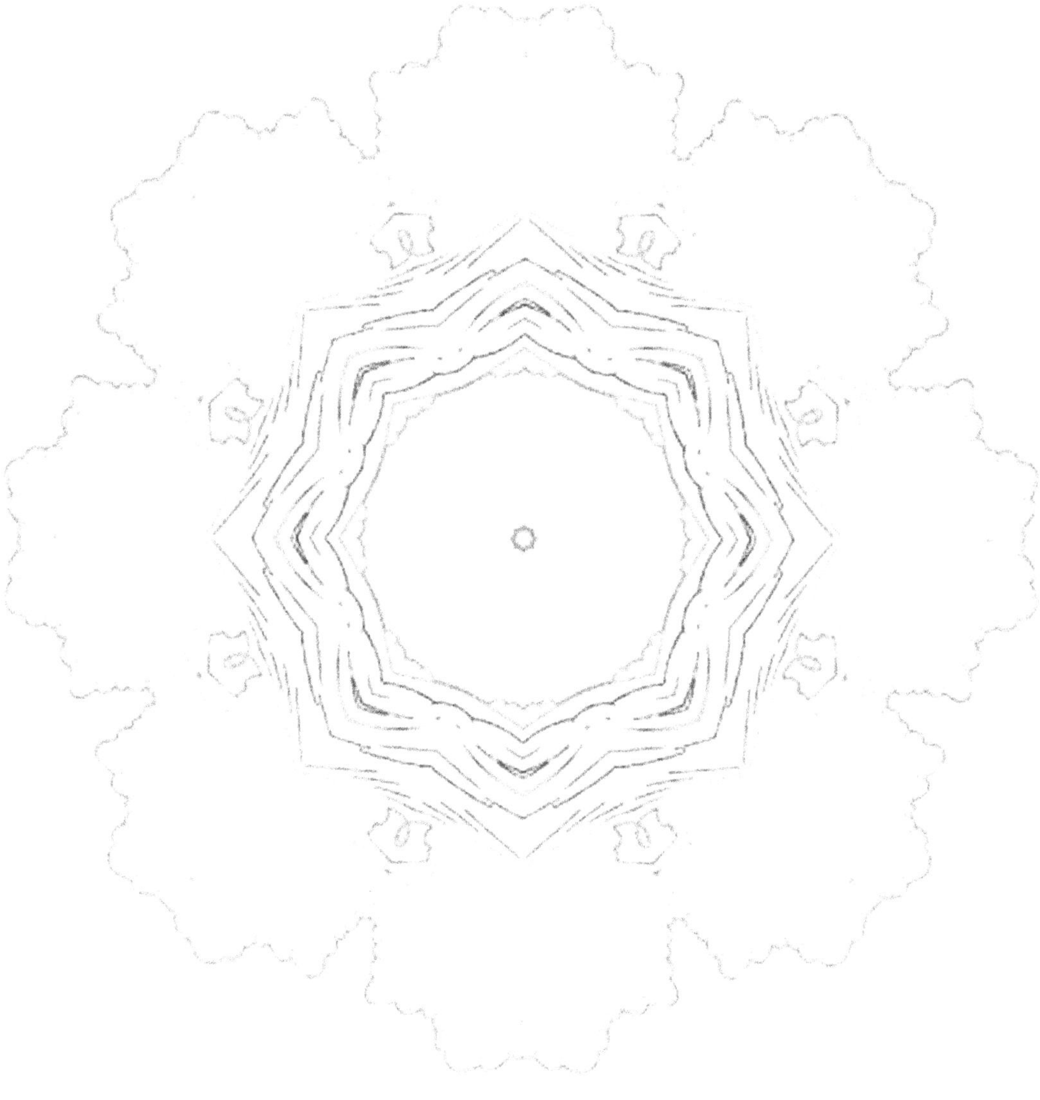

Note

www.ingramcontent.com/pod-product-compliance
Lightning Source LLC
Chambersburg PA
CBHW080649180526
45168CB00008B/3354